engineering eurekas

TUNNELS

Robyn Hardyman

PowerKiDS
press
New York

Published in 2017 by
The Rosen Publishing Group, Inc.
29 East 21st Street, New York, NY 10010

Cataloging-in-Publication Data

Names: Hardyman, Robyn.
Title: Tunnels / Robyn Hardyman.
Description: New York : PowerKids Press, 2017. | Series: Engineering eurekas | Includes index.
Identifiers: ISBN 9781499431094 (pbk.) | ISBN 9781499431117 (library bound) | ISBN 9781499431100 (6 pack)
Subjects: LCSH: Tunnels--Juvenile literature. | Tunnels--Design and construction--Juvenile literature.
Classification: LCC TA807.H349 2017 | DDC 624.1'93--dc23

Produced for Rosen by Calcium Creative Ltd
Editors for Calcium Creative Ltd: Sarah Eason and Harriet McGregor
Designers: Paul Myerscough and Jessica Moon
Picture researcher: Rachel Blount

Picture credits: Cover: Shutterstock: Tyler McKay. Inside: Venetia Dean 29 artwork; © AlpTransit Gotthard Ltd. 22–23b; Shutterstock: 52691989 20–21t, Paul Daniels 27b, Deatonphotos 18–19b, Everett Historical 15, Jeffrey M. Frank 10–11, GagliardiImages 17, Fer Gregory 11, Fat Jackey 18–19, Danger Jacobs 13b, Javarman 22–23t, Andre Nantel 4–5, Salajean 8–9, Sopotnicki 5, Oleg Totskyi 28, Xuanhuongho 14–15; Wikimedia Commons: AlMare 3, 6–7, Ariake 20–21b, Boerkevitz 9b, Patrick Cashin, Metropolitan Transportation Authority of the State of New York 26–27t, GeeKaa 21, Paul Hermans 16–17, NAEINSUN 7t, Lars Plougmann from United States 1, 12–13.

Manufactured in the United States of America

CPSIA Compliance Information: Batch #BW17PK: For Further Information contact Rosen Publishing, New York, New York at 1-800-237-9932.

Contents

A Natural Feature

Some tunnels are a natural feature of the landscape. They are carved out of rock very slowly, over hundreds of years, by wind and water. It may have been these natural tunnels that inspired people to build them. For thousands of years, people have built tunnels to carry water, other goods, and themselves underground. Through the centuries, **engineering** expertise has grown so we can now build spectacular tunnels.

Going Underground

In the state of Virginia, the Natural Tunnel began forming millions of years ago when a stream ran through the rock. Water seeped into cracks in the rock and gradually split it open. By the nineteenth century, the natural tunnel was big enough for a railroad! It is still in use today.

This natural tunnel was made underground when a flow of hot, melted rock called **lava** cooled on the outside and developed a solid crust. This created a tunnel for the rest of the lava to flow through, which was eventually left empty.

Man-made Tunnels

The earliest tunnels made by people date back thousands of years. The ancient Egyptians dug tunnels under their **monuments** in the Valley of the Kings. Between 2180 and 2160 BC, the ancient Babylonian people dug a tunnel under the Euphrates River. This was in an area named Mesopotamia, which today is Iraq. The tunnel was used to carry water from the river to the city. Other tunnels were built for defense. They provided a way of escaping secretly from enemies when under attack.

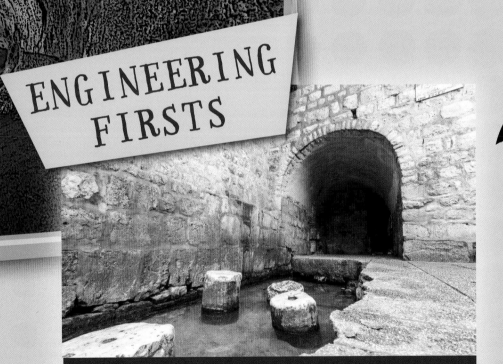

ENGINEERING FIRSTS

The Hezekiah Tunnel in Jerusalem is an amazing example of people's engineering skills thousands of years ago.

The Hezekiah Tunnel in the city of Jerusalem in Israel was dug in the 700s BC. It is about 1,750 feet (533 m) long. It carried water underground from a natural spring into the city. The people carved it out because they thought they were going to be attacked. They wanted a safe and secret supply of water. Water still runs through the S-shaped tunnel today, so they did a good job!

Built to Last

Over time, people learned more about tunnel engineering and they solved some of the problems of building them. Tunnels became bigger and better.

Ancient Engineering

The ancient Persians lived in a hot, dry land that today is Iran. They built networks of tunnels to carry water from rivers across the land so they could grow crops. This is called **irrigation**. The city of Gonabad in Iran still has a network of irrigation tunnels that were built 2,700 years ago by the ancient Persians.

The ancient Romans learned from the Persians, and used their technology. They also added new engineering of their own. They built tunnels to carry water, to take roads through mountains, and for mining. Sometimes, they built a tunnel starting from both ends, meeting in the middle to complete it. Modern engineers still do this today, but in Roman times it took much longer to tunnel through solid rock. The Romans built the Furlo Pass through a rocky hillside in northern Italy in AD 76. It was built to carry a road. It is 121 feet (37 m) long and 20 feet (6 m) high and is still in use today.

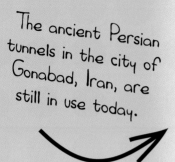

The ancient Persian tunnels in the city of Gonabad, Iran, are still in use today.

Thousands of years ago, the ancient Persians solved some of the key problems in building tunnels. They needed to get air to the people digging and remove the material they dug out. They placed posts across the surface of the land to show the course of the tunnel. Next, they dug straight down at each post. This created **shafts** for **ventilation** for the workers below. They were also used to remove the earth and rock. The shafts were then joined up below ground, creating the tunnel.

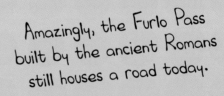

Amazingly, the Furlo Pass built by the ancient Romans still houses a road today.

Mines and Canals

One reason why people have always wanted to build tunnels is to mine, or dig for, valuable metals and **minerals** that lie deep underground. The engineering technology for reaching these precious materials has developed a lot over the centuries. The use of **gunpowder** made a huge difference to the engineering of tunnels. It was later used to help build **canals** for transporting goods.

Roman Mines

The Romans loved gold and other precious metals. There were sources of gold in parts of their empire, or lands, and they figured out how to mine it. One method was called fire quenching. They heated the rock with fire until it was very hot, then quickly cooled it with cold water. The sudden change in temperature caused the rock to crack. Workers then dug away the rock using the cracks. It was slow, difficult work and there was little ventilation for the miners.

This gold mine in Romania was created by the ancient Romans.

A "Breakthrough"

In the few centuries that followed, the technology did not move forward very much. Then, in the seventeenth century, a breakthrough came along with the invention of gunpowder. This explosive material could be set into rock and blast through it quickly. It was soon being used to tunnel into mines, though it made conditions very dangerous for the miners. Another new use for it was in building canals. The Erie Canal in New York State was completed in 1825, with one tunnel actually built under it!

ENGINEERING FIRSTS

In 1681, gunpowder was used on a large scale for the first time in an engineering project during the building of the Canal du Midi in Languedoc, in southern France. The canal is 150 miles (240 km) long and includes tunnels such as the 541-foot (165-m) Malpas Tunnel.

The Malpas Tunnel in France was Europe's first navigable canal tunnel.

The Railroad

In the nineteenth century, there was a new reason to build tunnels across the landscape: the railroad. This new means of transportation soon spread around the world, and so did the tunnels that carried the railroads through difficult **terrain**.

Blasting Through

Railroads cannot be built on steep slopes, so when a route hit a hill or mountain, the only solution was to tunnel through it. In Pennsylvania in 1831–1834, the first ever railroad tunnel in the United States was built for the Allegheny Portage Railroad. It was called the Staple Bend Tunnel and it was 901 feet (275 m) long. The tunnel was blasted from the Allegheny Mountains by drilling long holes and filling them with gunpowder. Work began at both ends, working toward the center. The tunnel grew by about 18 inches (46 cm) each day.

The Staple Bend Tunnel was given elaborate entrances to impress travelers. It is now a National Historic Landmark.

The invention of **dynamite** made it much easier to blast away rock when building tunnels.

In 1867, a Swedish engineer named Alfred Nobel (1833–1896) invented a new kind of explosive called dynamite. This was safer than earlier kinds of explosives. It soon led to a growth in tunnel construction around the world. Nobel also started the famous Nobel Prizes that are awarded to people who do groundbreaking work in the sciences, literature, and peace.

Longer and Longer

Railroads for steam trains were built everywhere. In the United Kingdom, a famous engineer named Isambard Kingdom Brunel (1806–1859) designed and built railroads, tunnels, bridges, and stations. For the Great Western Railway, he built the Box Tunnel in 1841. People thought it was impossible to build a tunnel long enough to go through Box Hill, but Brunel's tunnel was 1.83 miles (2.95 km) long. During construction, the only lighting was from candles. Blasting was done while workers were still underground, and about 100 men were killed during the project.

Crossing Rivers

When people want to cross a river, they usually build a bridge. It is more expensive to cross a river with an underground tunnel, but sometimes it is necessary. Tunneling underwater brings fresh challenges for engineers. The ground can be soft and may easily collapse. Flooding is also a real danger.

A Dangerous Mission

The first ever successful tunnel under a navigable river was the Thames Tunnel in London, England. Several attempts failed until an engineer named Marc Brunel (1769–1849) came up with the idea of an iron tunneling shield. This was a giant iron box that supported the roof of the tunnel as it was being made. This made it possible to tunnel through soft materials that would otherwise have collapsed. The tunnel was built from 1825–1843.

The workers could only dig a few inches at a time, because harmful gases filled the tunnel. If they drilled too close to the riverbed, the water rushed in. The tunnel flooded five times during construction, and several men were killed.

Clean Air

When tunnels were needed to take cars under rivers, engineers needed a solution to the problem of removing the vehicle exhaust fumes. The ventilation of tunnels was a big issue. In 1927, the Holland Tunnel under the Hudson River on the New York–New Jersey border opened. This was the first mechanically ventilated underwater tunnel in the world. To ventilate the tunnel, special buildings at each end of the tunnel housed 84 huge fans that changed the air inside the tunnel every 90 seconds.

The Thames Tunnel attracted millions of visitors when it opened in 1843. Today, it is used for trains.

FUTURE EUREKAS!

The technology used to ventilate the Holland Tunnel under the Hudson River has hardly changed today, and is sure to continue being used in the future. Because of this, the Holland Tunnel has been made a National Historic Civil and Mechanical Engineering Landmark.

Holland Tunnel
New Jersey
12'-6" CLEAR

The Holland Tunnel in New York is 1.6 miles (2.6 km) long.

Tunnels in War

Tunnels have always been used for defense. They provided secret underground escape routes from enemies, for example, during a **siege**. They have also been used in wartime for attack, to sneak up on an enemy and surprise them.

Battle of the Crater

During the American Civil War in 1864, **Union** forces spent several weeks digging a 510-foot (155 m) tunnel under a **Confederate** fort near Petersburg, Virginia. They supported it with timbers, filled it with gunpowder, and exploded it. This created a crater in the Confederate defenses. Union troops charged into this gap, but their fighting was not as skillful as their tunneling. The Battle of the Crater that followed lasted a long time and ended in defeat for the Union.

During the Vietnam War of 1955-1975 between the United States and North Vietnam, tunnels like this one were used by the North Vietnamese for hiding, communications, and carrying supplies.

Another War

Fifty years later, during World War I (1914–1918), tunneling engineers were at work again. The two sides, the Allies and the Central Powers, were fighting each other from **trenches** dug into the ground. The land between them was called "no man's land." Engineers on both sides dug tunnels under this land, toward the enemy trenches. They filled them with dynamite and exploded them, killing the enemy. These tunnels were amazing engineering achievements. They were dug in complete silence, so the enemy did not hear them coming.

ENGINEERING FIRSTS

In World War I, military engineers dug tunnels under the battlefields of the Somme region in France toward the enemy's lines.

During World War I, military tunneling techniques were forced to improve. By 1916, the British Army alone had about 25,000 trained tunnelers. Most of them had worked as coal miners before the war.

Getting Bigger

In the second half of the twentieth century, technology of all kinds advanced rapidly. As highways grew bigger and spread farther, road tunnels had to be wider and longer. Engineers found new ways to build these challenging structures.

Crossing the Bay

In 1936, in San Francisco, California, a tunnel was created that is still the widest single tunnel in the world. It measures 76 feet (23 m) wide and 58 feet (18 m) high. This was the Yerba Buena Island Tunnel. Drivers approach the tunnel by a bridge at one end. The tunnel then runs through the island, and a second bridge leaves it at the other end. The tunnel includes a double-deck roadway that is high enough to be used by large trucks.

Under New York

Another project was the series of Lincoln Tunnels in New York City. These three tunnels run under the Hudson River. They were designed by a Norwegian-American engineer named Ole Singstad (1882–1969). The first tunnel opened in 1937, the second and third in 1945 and 1957.

Each deck of the Yerba Buena Island Tunnel carries five lanes of traffic.

ENGINEERING FIRSTS

Whoo hoo!

Engineer Ole Singstad used and advanced the "sunk-tube" method of building underwater tunnels. This used 300-foot-long (90-m) sections of the tunnel that were **prefabricated**, or built elsewhere first. They were brought to the site and assembled in position. By 1950, Singstad had designed more underwater tunnels than any other engineer.

The three Lincoln Tunnels now carry hundreds of thousands of vehicles every day.

Cutting Through Rock

Creating a tunnel through rock by drilling and blasting was a slow and dangerous process, even with advances in engineering. Then, in 1952, a major breakthrough happened that made it possible to build the enormous tunnels that engineers are working on today.

The TBM

In 1952, James S. Robbins invented the modern **tunnel boring machine**, or TBM. The machine had been tried before. In 1853, an early TBM was used to dig the Hoosac Tunnel in Massachusetts, but it got stuck inside the mountain and was abandoned. Robbins' enormous new machine used sharp disks to cut through **shale** rock to create South Dakota's Oahe Dam.

The head of this massive tunnel boring machine is covered in sharp disks that cut through the ground.

The American Society of Civil Engineers named the Channel Tunnel one of the Seven Wonders of the Modern World.

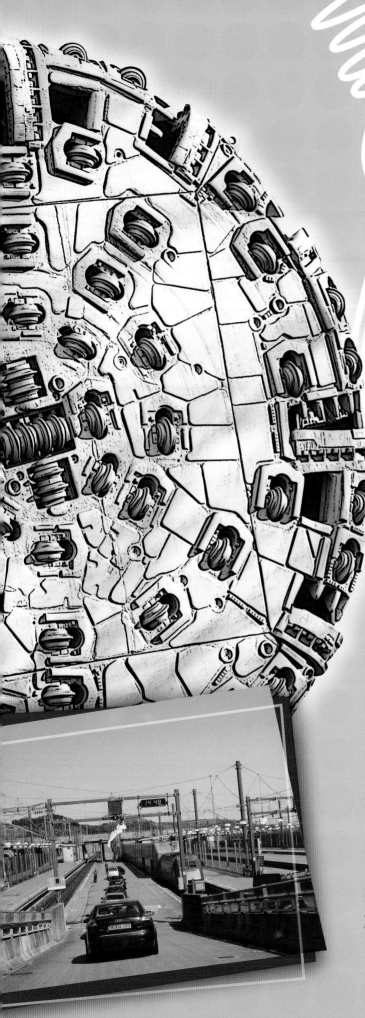

FUTURE EUREKAS!

The TBM used by James S. Robbins was the father of the machines in use today. They can bore through ground that is either hard or soft, and they create a tunnel with smooth, curved walls that can easily be lined. They work faster than drilling and blasting methods, too. This all reduces the cost of the tunnel.

Linking Two Countries

One of the greatest achievements of the tunneling world was completed in 1994. This was a tunnel to connect two nations, the United Kingdom and France, for the first time in history. It was dug under the English Channel and it stretches for 31 miles (50 km). The Channel Tunnel has three tunnels, two for trains traveling in both directions and a third as a "service" and emergency tunnel. It took TBMs three years to dig from each end until they finally met in the middle, deep below the seabed.

Finding a Way

Sometimes the location for a tunnel makes it impossible to use a TBM. It may be too difficult to access or the ground may not be suitable. In these situations, tunnel engineers must find new solutions.

A Chinese Wonder

The Guoliang Tunnel Road runs along the steep edge of a cliff of solid rock, in and out of the rock face through a series of mini tunnels. It took more than five years to chisel through the cliff to create this road, which opened in 1977. It is only 12 feet (3.7 m) wide, with a sheer drop to one side.

The "windows" cut out of the rock along the Guoliang Tunnel Road give stunning views into the valley way down below.

Japan decided to build its Seikan Tunnel when a violent typhoon sank five ferry boats making the crossing by sea, killing 1,430 people.

Connecting Islands

In 1988, another extraordinary tunnel opened that was built without a TBM—the Seikan Tunnel in Japan. The rock under the sea connecting the Japanese islands of Honshu and Hokkaido was not suitable for a TBM, so engineers used drilling and blasting. The finished tunnel is more than 33 miles (53 km) long. Until 2016, it was the longest railroad tunnel in the world. It is still the deepest, at 800 feet (244 m) below sea level.

ENGINEERING FIRSTS

These concrete tunnel sections were made off site before being sunk to their final positions in an underwater tunnel.

Another method of building tunnels underwater when a TBM cannot be used is the **immersed tube** method. Huge sections of the tunnel are made away from the site and then sunk into place in trenches underwater. Then they are connected. The tunnel pieces are made of either **steel** or **concrete**. Their ends are sealed to keep out the water.

Breaking New Ground

As engineers learned how to make bigger and better tunnels, they began to think about covering even longer distances. When these distances are over water, the best way to cover it is with a series of tunnels and bridges joined together. When a mountain is up ahead, the only way is through it.

Through Water

In 1997, the Tokyo Bay Aqua Line was opened. This was a 8.6-mile (13.8 km) tunnel-and-bridge combination across the bay. It reduced the driving time between the places at either end from 90 minutes to just 15 minutes. The tunnel part of the crossing begins on an artificial island in the bay, then runs below water for 6 miles (10 km).

Through Mountains

The longest road tunnel in the world is the 15-mile (24.5-km) Laerdal Tunnel in Norway, completed in 2000. This tunnel through the mountains is much safer than overland highways for drivers in Norway's freezing winters. The engineers designed three stopping places, or "caves," for drivers to rest.

In 2016, an even longer tunnel opened, in Switzerland. The Gotthard Base Tunnel runs for an incredible 35.4 miles (57 km) through the Alps Mountains and is the longest and deepest transportation tunnel in the world. It is a railroad tunnel and its purpose is to take passengers and **freight** off the roads. To make it, a TBM as long as four soccer fields cut away at the rock for more than 10 years.

The "cave" stopping places in the Laerdal Tunnel feature vivid blue and yellow lights.

More than 2,400 workers were involved in the construction of the record-breaking new Gotthard Base Tunnel through the Alps in Switzerland.

FUTURE EUREKAS!

In Boston, Massachusetts, a project to bury the main highway in a massive tunnel presented the engineers with a great challenge. The lessons they learned from it will drive inner-city tunnel building in the future. The Central Artery/Tunnel was completed in 2007, surrounded by skyscrapers and highways.

Global Tunnels

ASIA

NORTH AMERICA

Tokyo Bay Aqua Line, Japan, 6 miles (10 km)

Yerba Buena Island Tunnel, San Francisco, California, 76 feet (24 m) wide and 58 feet (18 m) high

Seikan Tunnel, Japan, 33.5 miles (53.8 km)

How do engineers tunnel through soft ground under a sea or riverbed and support the tunnel as they go?

Can you think of some advantages of having a highway travel through a tunnel rather than over land? Think about the effect on the local area, the journey time, and safety issues.

AUSTRALIA

How do engineers cross wide expanses of water in modern projects?

How do you think the invention of the tunnel improved people's lives? Give your reasons.

Laerdal Tunnel, Norway, 15 miles (24.5 km)

Channel Tunnel, England-France, 31 miles (50 km)

Central Artery/Tunnel Project, Boston, Massachusetts, 3.5 miles (5.6 km)

EUROPE

Gotthard Base Tunnel, Switzerland, 35.4 miles (57 km)

Delaware Aqueduct bypass tunnel, New York City, 85 miles (137 km)

AFRICA

Lincoln Tunnels, New York City, 1.5 miles (2.4 km)

SOUTH AMERICA

Today's tunnel projects take many years to complete and often cost billions of dollars. Do you think they are worth it?

Tunnels of the Future

There is no doubt that we will continue to build amazing tunnels in the future. There are some large-scale projects underway around the world today, with many more planned for the future.

New York City

The longest tunnel in the world does not carry transportation. It is the Delaware Aqueduct, an 85-mile (137 km) tunnel that carries the water supply to New York City. It was drilled through solid rock in the 1940s, and it is leaking. Engineers are working on an enormous new tunnel below the Hudson River to take the water away from the leakiest areas of the old tunnel so they can be fixed. This complex project should be completed in 2021.

Another major project in New York City is the East Side Access Project. Engineers are digging through rock below the city to create new subway lines and stations to bring thousands of workers into the city every day. It is scheduled for completion in 2019, at a cost of $15 billion.

The rock below the streets of New York City is being tunneled away for the new subway line.

In 2013, the world's largest TBM began work to replace the highway on the Alaskan Way Viaduct in Seattle, Washington, with a new underground highway. This massive machine weighs 7,000 tons (6,350 mt) and is 57.5 feet (17.5 m) wide. The future will definitely see machines like this one carving out the tunnels we need.

Crossing London

In London, the Crossrail project is one of the biggest tunneling operations in Europe. Crossrail will be a new railroad that runs under London. A huge tunnel is being dug below central London for the tracks, while life in the city carries on as normal. Crossrail is due to open in 2018.

The new tunnels for the Crossrail project in London are lined with concrete.

A Connected World

We have come a long way from the first tunnels built to carry water and for defense. We still use tunnels to carry our water, but we also need them to carry transportation. Our highways and railroads need tunnels like never before.

More Transportation

The development of railroads and motor vehicles in the nineteenth and twentieth centuries led to a huge expansion in tunnel building. Tunnels around the world were built to carry tracks and highways. Today and into the future, not even mountains and oceans can stand in the way of tunnel engineers. The challenges of making a tunnel are the same as they ever were: how to cut through the ground, how to support the tunnel, and how to bring fresh air into it. The solutions, however, have become ever more complex.

Modern subway tunnels are very complex engineering projects.

Be an Engineer

You can find out for yourself some of the problems that tunnel engineers have to solve with this simple activity.

You Will Need:
- Modeling clay
- Popsicle sticks
- A pencil
- A plastic spoon
- A cardboard tube 1.5 inches (3.8 cm) in diameter
- Books or other heavy objects

- Make a "mountain" out of modeling clay, at least 4 inches (10 cm) square at the base and 4 inches (10 cm) high. Stand it on a flat surface.

- Now try to find the best tools for boring your tunnel through the mountain. It should be at least 1.5 inches (3.8 cm) wide. Try sticking the Popsicle sticks straight into it. Then try digging out the clay with the plastic spoon. Finally, try twisting the pencil into it.

- How about starting your tunnel from both ends, and meeting in the middle?

- When your tunnel is complete, insert a tube into it for extra support. Now test your tunnel by resting heavy books on the mountain. Is your tunnel strong enough to take their weight?

Glossary

canals Man-made waterways.

concrete A mixture of sand, stones, cement, and water.

Confederate The side of the Southern states in the Civil War.

crater A large dip or hole in the ground caused by an explosion.

deck A highway that is raised and supported.

dynamite An explosive material that is safer than pure gunpowder.

engineering The branch of science having to do with the design of structures.

freight Transported goods.

gunpowder An explosive.

immersed tube A method of building tunnels underwater using large pieces made off-site and lowered into the water to be joined together.

irrigation A system of carrying water to fields for growing crops.

lava Hot melted rock.

minerals Substances found in the ground.

monuments Buildings or statues.

navigable Deep and clear enough to be used by boats.

prefabricated Made in a factory and brought to a site to be assembled.

shafts Deep and narrow holes.

shale A soft rock that is easily split into pieces.

siege When a place is surrounded by enemies to force it to surrender.

steel A strong metal made from iron and carbon.

terrain A stretch of land.

trenches Long, narrow holes cut into the ground.

tunnel boring machine (TBM) A huge circular machine used to tunnel through the ground.

tunneling shield A structure that supports the roof of a tunnel as it is being dug out of soft material.

Union The side of the Northern states in the Civil War.

ventilation A system for getting fresh air into and out of a space.

Further Reading

Books

Kalle, Stuart A. *Great Idea: The Chunnel*. Chicago, IL:
Norwood House Press, 2013.

Latham, Donna. *Bridges and Tunnels: Investigate Feats of Engineering*.
White River Junction, VT: Nomad Press, 2012.

Mattern, Joanne. *Tunnels*. Vero Beach, FL:
Rourke Educational Media, 2015.

Price, Jane. *Underworld: Exploring the World Beneath Your Feet*.
Boston, MA: Kids Can Press, 2014.

Websites

Due to the changing nature of Internet links, PowerKids Press has
developed an online list of websites related to the subject of this book.
This site is updated regularly. Please use this link to access the list:

www.powerkidslinks.com/ee/tunnels

Index